AF416923

Appalachian Nightmares: The Top 10 Creepy Creatures of the Mountains

Edward Turner

Published by Oliver Lancaster, 2023.

While every precaution has been taken in the preparation of this book, the publisher assumes no responsibility for errors or omissions, or for damages resulting from the use of the information contained herein.

APPALACHIAN NIGHTMARES: THE TOP 10 CREEPY CREATURES OF THE MOUNTAINS

First edition. July 8, 2023.

Copyright © 2023 Edward Turner.

ISBN: 979-8223932017

Written by Edward Turner.

Also by Edward Turner

Ghosts of Paris: Ten Haunted Places in the City of Love
Appalachian Nightmares: The Top 10 Creepy Creatures of the Mountains
Asia's Top Ten Cryptids: Legends, Sightings, and Theories
Evil Women in History: Uncovering the Gruesome Crimes of Ten Notorious Female Killers
Ghosts of London: Ten Haunted Places in The City
Ghosts of New York: Ten Haunted Places in The Big Apple
Missouri Nightmares: The Top 10 Chilling Legends
North America's Top Ten Cryptids: Legends, Sightings, and Theories

Appalachian Nightmares: The Top 10 Creepy Creatures of the Mountains

Introduction

Folklore and its significance in the Appalachian region

The historical and cultural context

Horror and supernatural stories in popular culture

Chapter 1: The Smoke Wolf

The origin and history of the Smoke Wolf legend

Sightings

Chapter 2: The Silver Giant

The origin and history

The Silver Giant in folklore and mythology

An omen of death and its cultural implications

Chapter 3: The Raven Mocker

The origin and history

The Cherokee mythology

Chapter 4: The Virginia Devil Monkey

The origin and history

The cultural significance

APPALACHIAN NIGHTMARES: THE TOP 10 CREEPY CREATURES OF THE MOUNTAINS

Historical sightings and encounters

Chapter 5: The Dwayyo

The origin and history

Folklore and pop culture

Psychological implications

Chapter 6: The Bell Witch

The origin and history

Cultural significance

Evidence

Chapter 7: The Flatwoods Monster

The origin and history

Other extraterrestrial creatures in folklore

The social and political implications during the Cold War era

Chapter 8: The Wampus Cat

The origin and history

Cherokee folklore surrounding the Wampus Cat

Folklore and mythology

The impact on the Appalachian community

Chapter 9: The Grafton Monster

The origin and history

Historical sightings and encounters

Scientific explanations

Chapter 10: The Snallygaster

The origin and history

The historical sightings and encounters

Physical appearance and behaviour

The cultural significance

Conclusion

APPALACHIAN NIGHTMARES: THE TOP 10 CREEPY CREATURES OF THE MOUNTAINS

Introduction

Folklore and its significance in the Appalachian region

Folklore is a term that encompasses a wide range of cultural traditions, including myths, legends, stories, customs, beliefs, and practices that are passed down from generation to generation through oral or written communication. It is a vital aspect of human culture and has played a crucial role in shaping the beliefs, values, and customs of societies across the world.

The Appalachian region, which stretches across the eastern United States from Georgia to Pennsylvania, has a rich and diverse folklore tradition that reflects the unique history and culture of the region. The Appalachian Mountains have been home to a variety of peoples and cultures, including Native American tribes, European settlers, and African Americans, each of whom has contributed to the rich tapestry of Appalachian folklore.

One of the most important functions of folklore is to provide a sense of identity and belonging to a community. In the Appalachian region, folklore has played a crucial role in shaping the cultural identity of the people who live there. Stories, songs, and other forms of folklore have been used to pass down traditions and values from one generation to the next, helping to create a sense of continuity and connection to the past.

One of the most significant forms of Appalachian folklore is storytelling. The tradition of storytelling has been an integral part of Appalachian culture for centuries, and stories have been used to teach lessons, pass down knowledge, and entertain audiences of all ages. Many of these stories are steeped in Appalachian history and culture, featuring characters and themes that reflect the unique experiences of the people who live in the region.

Another important aspect of Appalachian folklore is music. Music has been a central part of Appalachian culture since the earliest days of European settlement, and the region has produced a rich tradition of ballads, hymns, and other types of music. Many of these songs are steeped in the history and culture of the region, and they reflect the struggles and triumphs of the Appalachian people.

In addition to storytelling and music, Appalachian folklore also includes a wide range of beliefs and customs. These beliefs and customs reflect the unique worldview of the Appalachian people, and they often have roots in the region's natural environment. For example, many Appalachian beliefs and customs are centred around the mountains, forests, and rivers that are so central to life in the region.

One of the most important functions of Appalachian folklore is to provide a sense of connection to the natural world. The Appalachian Mountains are home to a rich and diverse ecosystem, and the people who live in the region have developed a deep respect and appreciation for the natural world. Many Appalachian folktales feature animals, plants, and other elements of nature as central characters, reflecting the close relationship between the people of the region and their environment.

The historical and cultural context

THE APPALACHIAN REGION is a unique and diverse cultural landscape that has been shaped by its history and geography. The region stretches from Georgia to Pennsylvania and encompasses a wide range of landscapes, from the rolling hills and valleys of the Piedmont to the rugged peaks of the Blue Ridge Mountains.

The Appalachian region has a rich history that dates back thousands of years. The area was first inhabited by various Native American tribes, including the Cherokee, Creek, and Shawnee. These tribes developed their own unique cultures and traditions, which were passed down from generation to generation through oral storytelling and other forms of communication.

In the late 18th and early 19th centuries, the Appalachian region saw an influx of European settlers, who brought with them their own cultural traditions and beliefs. These settlers came from a wide range of countries, including England, Scotland, Ireland, and Germany, and they brought with them their own customs, music, and storytelling traditions.

The unique cultural mix of Native American, European, and African American traditions helped to shape the development of Appalachian folklore and mythology. These traditions were influenced by the harsh realities of life in the region, including poverty, isolation, and a rugged natural environment.

One of the most important aspects of Appalachian folklore is its connection to the natural world. The Appalachian Mountains are home to a wide range of plants and animals, and the people who live in the region have developed a deep respect and appreciation for the natural world. Many Appalachian folktales feature animals, plants, and other elements of nature as central characters, reflecting the close relationship between the people of the region and their environment.

Another important aspect of Appalachian folklore is its connection to the region's history and cultural traditions. Appalachian folklore often reflects the struggles and triumphs of the people who live in the region, including their experiences with poverty, disease, and other challenges. Many Appalachian folktales feature heroic characters who overcome adversity and triumph over their enemies, reflecting the resilience and determination of the Appalachian people.

Music is also an important aspect of Appalachian folklore. The region has a rich musical heritage that includes traditional ballads, hymns, and other forms of music. Appalachian music reflects the diverse cultural traditions of the region, and it has been influenced by a wide range of musical styles, including English, Scottish, Irish, and African American.

Overall, the Appalachian region is a unique and diverse cultural landscape that has been shaped by its history, geography, and the diverse mix of cultural traditions that have been brought to the region over the centuries. Appalachian folklore and mythology reflect the struggles and triumphs of the people who live in the region, and they provide a powerful connection to the natural world and the region's rich cultural heritage.

Horror and supernatural stories in popular culture

HORROR AND SUPERNATURAL stories have been a popular form of entertainment for centuries. From ancient folklore and mythology to modern-day horror movies and TV shows, people have always been drawn to stories that explore the darker aspects of the human experience.

One reason for the enduring popularity of horror and supernatural stories is their ability to tap into our deepest fears and anxieties. These stories often deal with themes of death, loss, and the unknown, which are universal human experiences that we all must confront at some point in our lives. By exploring these themes in a fictional setting, horror and supernatural stories allow us to confront our fears in a safe and controlled environment.

Another reason for the enduring popularity of horror and supernatural stories is their ability to provide a sense of escapism. For many people, horror and supernatural stories offer a way to temporarily escape from the stresses and anxieties of everyday life by immersing themselves in a fictional world filled with monsters, ghosts, and other supernatural creatures.

The Appalachian Nightmares framework fits into this tradition by offering a collection of terrifying stories that draw on the rich folklore and mythology of the Appalachian region. Each chapter explores a different creature or legend, ranging from werewolves and poltergeists to giant humanoid creatures and winged monsters.

Like other horror and supernatural stories, the Appalachian Nightmares framework taps into our deepest fears and anxieties. Many of the creatures and legends featured in the framework reflect the harsh realities of life in the Appalachian region, including poverty, disease, and isolation. By exploring these themes through the lens of supernatural horror, the framework allows us to confront our fears in a safe and controlled environment.

At the same time, the Appalachian Nightmares framework also offers a sense of escapism. By immersing ourselves in the world of Appalachian folklore and mythology, we can temporarily escape from the stresses and anxieties of everyday life and explore a world filled with terrifying creatures and supernatural beings.

Overall, the enduring popularity of horror and supernatural stories can be attributed to their ability to tap into our deepest fears and anxieties while also providing a sense of escapism. The Appalachian Nightmares framework fits into this tradition by offering a collection of terrifying stories that draw on the rich

APPALACHIAN NIGHTMARES: THE TOP 10 CREEPY CREATURES OF THE MOUNTAINS

folklore and mythology of the Appalachian region, allowing us to confront our fears and escape into a world of supernatural horror.

EDWARD TURNER

Chapter 1: The Smoke Wolf

The origin and history of the Smoke Wolf legend

The Smoke Wolf is a legendary creature that is said to haunt the forests of Appalachia. It is known for leaving behind a trail of smoke and terror, and its origins can be traced back to the rich folklore and mythology of the region.

The legend of the Smoke Wolf has its roots in the Native American tribes that once inhabited the Appalachian region. According to their folklore, the Smoke Wolf was a powerful spirit that protected the forests and the animals that lived there. It was said to be a shape-shifter, able to take on the form of both a wolf and a human, and was revered by the Native Americans as a powerful guardian spirit.

Over time, the legend of the Smoke Wolf evolved and became intertwined with European folklore. As European settlers began to populate the Appalachian region, they brought with them their own legends and superstitions, many of which were related to wolves and other wild animals.

One popular theory is that the Smoke Wolf legend was influenced by the legend of the Wild Hunt, a European folktale that tells of a spectral pack of hounds led by a supernatural hunter. The Wild Hunt was said to ride through the night sky, chasing after lost souls and causing chaos wherever it went. It is possible that the Smoke Wolf legend was inspired by this European folktale, with the wolf-like creature taking on the role of the spectral hunter.

As the Smoke Wolf legend continued to evolve, it became associated with other supernatural phenomena, such as mysterious fires and unexplained smoke. It was said that the Smoke Wolf would leave behind a trail of smoke wherever it went, and that this smoke was a sign of impending doom or tragedy.

In the late 19th and early 20th centuries, the legend of the Smoke Wolf gained renewed popularity thanks to the emergence of the American folklore movement. Folklorists and collectors began to travel throughout the Appalachian region, gathering stories and legends from the local people. The Smoke Wolf legend was one of the many stories that was recorded and passed down through the generations.

Today, the Smoke Wolf legend continues to be a popular part of Appalachian folklore. It has been featured in numerous books, movies, and TV shows, and is often cited as an example of the rich cultural heritage of the region. Despite the passage of time, the legend of the Smoke Wolf remains a powerful reminder of the enduring power of myth and legend in our lives.

Sightings

SIGHTINGS OF THE SMOKE Wolf, also known as the Smoke Dog or the Smoker, have been reported for centuries throughout the Appalachian region. Though many people dismiss the legend as nothing more than a tall tale, there are those who claim to have seen the creature with their own eyes.

Descriptions of the Smoke Wolf vary, but most accounts describe a large, wolf-like creature with smoky fur that seems to trail behind it like a cloud. It is said to move quickly and silently through the forest, leaving behind a trail of smoke and an eerie feeling of dread.

One of the earliest recorded sightings of the Smoke Wolf comes from the journal of a French explorer named Pierre Francois Xavier de Charlevoix. In 1721, de Charlevoix was travelling through what is now West Virginia when he encountered a group of Native Americans who told him of a creature that they called the "Smoke Dog." According to the Native Americans, the Smoke Dog was a powerful spirit that guarded the forest and could change shape at will.

In more recent times, sightings of the Smoke Wolf have become less common, but there are still those who claim to have seen the creature. One such sighting occurred in 1963, when a group of hunters in Pennsylvania reported seeing a large, smoky animal that they couldn't identify. The creature reportedly moved quickly through the woods and disappeared before the hunters could get a closer look.

Another sighting occurred in 1977, when a man in Kentucky claimed to have seen a large, wolf-like creature that left behind a trail of smoke. The man said that the creature seemed to be watching him and his hunting dog from a distance, but disappeared as soon as they approached.

Perhaps the most famous sighting of the Smoke Wolf occurred in 1994, when a group of hikers in West Virginia claimed to have seen the creature up close. The hikers reported that the Smoke Wolf was about the size of a large dog, but had a smoky, almost translucent appearance. The creature reportedly stared at the hikers for several moments before disappearing into the woods.

Despite the numerous sightings of the Smoke Wolf, there is little scientific evidence to support the existence of such a creature. Many sceptics believe that the legend is simply a product of the rich folklore and mythology of the Appalachian region, and that the sightings can be explained by other natural phenomena.

Regardless of whether the Smoke Wolf is real or simply a legend, it continues to capture the imagination of people throughout the Appalachian region and beyond. Its eerie appearance and mysterious nature have made it a popular subject of books, movies, and TV shows, and it remains one of the most enduring legends of the area.

APPALACHIAN NIGHTMARES: THE TOP 10 CREEPY CREATURES OF THE MOUNTAINS

Chapter 2: The Silver Giant

The origin and history

The Silver Giant, also known as the Appalachian Giant or the Mountain Giant, is a legendary creature said to roam the mountains of Appalachia. Descriptions of the Silver Giant vary, but most accounts describe a towering humanoid figure with silver or grey skin and enormous size, often reaching heights of up to 10 feet tall.

The origin of the Silver Giant legend is unclear, but some scholars believe that it may have been inspired by Native American myths and legends. Many Native American tribes, including the Cherokee and the Iroquois, have their own stories of giant creatures that lived in the mountains and forests.

One such legend tells of a powerful being called Stonecoat, who was said to be a giant with a coat made of stone. According to the story, Stonecoat could control the weather and had the power to heal the sick and injured. Another legend tells of a race of giants who lived in the mountains and were feared by the Native Americans who lived nearby.

As European settlers began to move into the Appalachian region in the 18th century, they brought with them their own stories and myths of giants and other supernatural creatures.

Some of these tales may have contributed to the development of the Silver Giant legend.

One early account of the Silver Giant comes from a man named Henry Clay, who claimed to have encountered the creature in the early 19th century. According to Clay, he was travelling through the mountains when he came upon a giant figure with silver skin and glowing eyes. The creature reportedly towered over Clay and emitted a loud, unearthly roar before disappearing into the woods.

In the decades that followed, numerous other sightings of the Silver Giant were reported throughout the Appalachian region. Some people claimed to have seen the creature walking through the woods or standing atop a mountain peak, while others reported hearing its loud, booming footsteps in the distance.

The Silver Giant also became a popular subject of folklore and mythology in the region. Many people believed that the creature was a guardian of the mountains and forests, and that it protected the area from harm. Others believed that the Silver Giant was a harbinger of death and disaster, and that its appearance signalled a coming tragedy.

Despite the numerous sightings and stories, there is little scientific evidence to support the existence of the Silver Giant. Many sceptics believe that the legend is simply a product of the rich folklore and mythology of the Appalachian region, and that the sightings can be explained by other natural phenomena.

Regardless of whether the Silver Giant is real or simply a legend, it remains a popular subject of fascination and intrigue in the Appalachian region and beyond. Its enormous size, silver skin, and otherworldly appearance have captured the imaginations of people for centuries, and the legend of the Silver Giant shows no signs of fading away.

The Silver Giant in folklore and mythology

THE SILVER GIANT IS a towering creature of Appalachian folklore, said to be a guardian of the mountains and an omen of death. It is not alone in the realm of giant creatures in mythology, as there are many other examples of massive beings that have captured the imagination of people around the world. In this essay, we will compare and contrast the Silver Giant to other giant creatures in folklore and mythology.

One of the most famous giant creatures in mythology is the Cyclops. In Greek mythology, the Cyclops was a one-eyed giant that was said to have been born to the god Uranus and the goddess Gaia. They were known for their strength and ability to forge weapons and tools, which they used to great effect in battles with the gods and heroes of ancient Greece. The Cyclops was also known for their fierce and independent spirit, which sometimes led them to challenge the gods themselves.

In contrast, the Silver Giant is said to be a more benevolent creature, a guardian of the mountains that helps to protect the natural beauty of the Appalachian region. While the Cyclops was often portrayed as a destructive force that could be difficult to control, the Silver Giant is seen as a protector of nature and a symbol of the power and majesty of the mountains.

Another giant creature in mythology that bears some similarities to the Silver Giant is the Jotun, a race of giants from Norse mythology. The Jotun were said to be fierce and powerful beings, often living in the mountains and other wild places. They were known for their strength and cunning, and were often seen as a threat to the gods themselves.

Like the Silver Giant, the Jotun were associated with the natural world and were often depicted as protectors of the land and its creatures. They were also seen as embodiments of chaos and the forces of nature, which could be both destructive and life-giving.

One more example of a giant creature in mythology is the Oni of Japanese folklore. Oni are often depicted as huge and fearsome creatures with horns and sharp teeth, and are said to be capable of causing great destruction and chaos. They are often seen as malevolent beings that seek to do harm to humans, although they can also be tricked or defeated by clever heroes.

In contrast, the Silver Giant is not seen as a malevolent or destructive force, but rather as a symbol of the natural world and its beauty and power. While the Oni is often seen as a frightening and dangerous creature, the Silver Giant is more often portrayed as a benevolent and awe-inspiring figure that inspires respect and admiration.

The Silver Giant is a unique and fascinating figure in the world of mythology and folklore, and shares many similarities and differences with other giant creatures from around the world. While some giant creatures are seen as malevolent and destructive, the Silver Giant is a symbol of the natural world and its beauty and power, and is often portrayed as a protector of the mountains and their inhabitants.

An omen of death and its cultural implications

THE SILVER GIANT IS a towering humanoid creature that is said to inhabit the Appalachian Mountains. According to legend, encountering the Silver Giant is an omen of impending death, and its appearance is said to signal the approach of doom and destruction. The significance of the Silver Giant as an omen of death is deeply rooted in the cultural history of the Appalachian region and reflects the region's history, traditions, and beliefs.

One of the most striking aspects of the Silver Giant legend is its connection to death and destruction. In many cultures, the presence of giant creatures is often associated with danger and foreboding. This is particularly true in the case of the Silver Giant, which is said to be a harbinger of death and disaster. The legend of the Silver Giant speaks to the deep-seated fears of the people who inhabit the Appalachian Mountains and reflects their concerns about the fragility of life in a harsh and unforgiving landscape.

At the same time, the Silver Giant legend is also a reflection of the region's cultural heritage. The Appalachian Mountains have a rich history that is rooted in the traditions of the people who have lived there for generations. These traditions are deeply intertwined with the natural world, and the folklore and mythology of the region reflect this connection. The legend of the Silver Giant is just one example of how the people of the Appalachian Mountains have used storytelling and folklore to make sense of their world.

One way in which the Silver Giant legend reflects the cultural heritage of the Appalachian region is through its connection to the natural world. The legend describes the Silver Giant as a guardian of the forests and mountains of Appalachia, a being who is intimately connected to the land and its creatures. This connection to the natural world is a recurring theme in Appalachian folklore, and reflects the region's deep respect for the natural world and the creatures that inhabit it.

Another way in which the Silver Giant legend reflects the cultural heritage of the Appalachian region is through its connection to history and tradition. The legend of the Silver Giant is not a recent invention, but has been passed down through generations of Appalachian storytellers. This tradition of storytelling is deeply ingrained in the culture of the region and reflects the importance of oral history in the Appalachian Mountains.

Finally, the Silver Giant legend also reflects the resilience and resourcefulness of the people who inhabit the Appalachian Mountains. The legend describes a creature that is powerful and fearsome, but also vulnerable to the forces of nature and the passage of time. This theme of resilience and resourcefulness is a recurring theme in Appalachian folklore and reflects the region's history of overcoming adversity and hardship.

The legend of the Silver Giant is a fascinating example of the power of folklore and mythology to reflect the cultural heritage of a region. The legend's connection to death and destruction speaks to the fears and concerns of the people who inhabit the Appalachian Mountains, while its connection to the natural world reflects the region's deep respect for the land and its creatures. The legend also reflects the importance of storytelling and oral history in the Appalachian region and the resilience and resourcefulness of the people who call it home.

EDWARD TURNER

Chapter 3: The Raven Mocker

The origin and history

The Raven Mocker is a malevolent shapeshifting creature found in the folklore of several Native American tribes, including the Cherokee, Creek, and Choctaw. This legendary creature is believed to have the ability to transform into a large bird, usually a raven, and is known to be a harbinger of death and disease.

The Raven Mocker is thought to be an evil spirit that preys on the sick and dying. According to legend, the creature is able to sense when someone is close to death and will fly to their bedside, either to hasten their death or to steal their life force. The Raven Mocker is said to have sharp claws and a piercing beak that it uses to tear out the hearts of its victims. It is also believed to have a powerful voice that it uses to call out the name of its intended victim, driving them to madness before they die.

The origins of the Raven Mocker legend are difficult to trace, as it is part of the oral tradition of many different tribes. However, some scholars believe that the legend may have originated in the Cherokee tribe, as the creature is often associated with Cherokee death rituals.

In Cherokee mythology, the Raven Mocker is said to be a witch who has acquired the power of flight by consuming the heart of a freshly deceased human. The witch then uses this power to fly around at night, seeking out the sick and dying. The Cherokee believe that the Raven Mocker can only be killed by discovering its true identity, which is said to be hidden somewhere on its body.

The legend of the Raven Mocker has been passed down through generations of Native American tribes, and it remains an important part of their cultural heritage. It has also been incorporated into mainstream American culture, appearing in novels, films, and television shows.

In recent years, the Raven Mocker has become a popular subject of study among scholars of Native American folklore. Some researchers believe that the legend may have originated as a way for Native American tribes to cope with the high mortality rates brought on by disease and warfare. Others suggest that the legend may have served as a way for tribes to reinforce the importance of respecting the dead and dying.

Despite its dark and ominous reputation, the Raven Mocker remains a fascinating and enduring legend that continues to capture the imaginations of people around the world. Whether it is seen as a symbol of death and disease, or as a warning against the dangers of unchecked power, the Raven Mocker remains an important part of the cultural heritage of many Native American tribes.

The Cherokee mythology

THE CHEROKEE PEOPLE have a rich mythology and belief system that has influenced many of the legends and folklore in the Appalachian region, including the Raven Mocker. According to Cherokee mythology, the Raven is a powerful spirit that has the ability to shape shift and take on different forms. The Raven is often associated with death, transformation, and the spirit world, and is revered as a powerful guide and protector.

The Raven Mocker legend draws heavily from Cherokee mythology, particularly the belief in the "tsi-sgili," or "spirit witches." In Cherokee tradition, these witches are believed to be powerful sorcerers who have the ability to shapeshift into various forms, including that of a giant bird like the Raven. They are often associated with death and are said to prey on the sick and dying, stealing their life force and causing them to waste away.

The Raven Mocker legend tells the story of a witch who has mastered the art of shapeshifting and has taken on the form of a giant bird, specifically the Raven. The Raven Mocker is said to prey on the sick and dying, stealing their life force and prolonging their own life. According to legend, the Raven Mocker can only be killed by uncovering its true identity, which is believed to be hidden somewhere on its body.

Cherokee mythology also plays a significant role in the methods used to protect oneself from the Raven Mocker. The Cherokee people believe that the Raven Mocker can be detected by the sound of its wings, which make a distinct flapping noise. To ward off the Raven Mocker, the Cherokee would often use various protective measures, such as hanging up gourds or other objects that would make noise when disturbed. They would also use charms and amulets to protect themselves and their loved ones from the Raven Mocker's attacks.

The Raven Mocker legend has continued to be a popular and enduring part of Appalachian folklore, inspiring countless stories, books, and films. Its ties to Cherokee mythology have helped to preserve this important aspect of Cherokee culture and tradition. Today, many Cherokee communities still celebrate their heritage and beliefs through storytelling and other cultural practices, ensuring that the legacy of the Raven Mocker and other Cherokee legends will continue for generations to come.

APPALACHIAN NIGHTMARES: THE TOP 10 CREEPY CREATURES OF THE MOUNTAINS

Chapter 4: The Virginia Devil Monkey

The origin and history

The Virginia Devil Monkey is a cryptid creature that is said to roam the Appalachian Mountains. Described as a hybrid of a primate and a devil, this creature has been a part of Appalachian folklore for generations. Its origins and history are shrouded in mystery, but many believe that it has been a part of the region's folklore for centuries.

The first known sighting of the Virginia Devil Monkey was in the late 1950s, when several people reported seeing a strange creature in the woods near the town of Fauquier. According to these witnesses, the creature was about four feet tall, covered in black fur, and had a head that resembled that of a dog or a baboon. It was said to have red eyes and long claws on its fingers and toes. Some even claimed that it had wings like a bat.

Since that initial sighting, reports of the Virginia Devil Monkey have been sporadic but persistent. There have been numerous sightings of the creature throughout Virginia and other Appalachian states, including West Virginia, Kentucky, and North Carolina. Witnesses describe the creature as being aggressive and territorial, and many believe that it is a harbinger of doom and destruction.

The origins of the Virginia Devil Monkey legend are unclear. Some believe that it is a creature that was brought to the region by early European settlers, who may have imported exotic animals for entertainment or for use in medical experiments. Others believe that it is a creature that has always been a part of Appalachian folklore, passed down from generation to generation through oral tradition.

One theory about the Virginia Devil Monkey's origin is that it is a descendent of a prehistoric primate known as the Protopithecus. This theory suggests that the creature may have survived in the remote mountains of the Appalachians, evolving over time into the cryptid creature that is known today.

The Virginia Devil Monkey has also been associated with other supernatural phenomena, such as UFO sightings and other cryptid creatures like Bigfoot. Some believe that the creature is an extraterrestrial or a product of genetic experimentation, while others see it as a manifestation of dark forces or demonic entities.

Despite its elusive nature and uncertain origins, the Virginia Devil Monkey remains a popular figure in Appalachian folklore and has even made its way into popular culture. It has been featured in books, movies, and TV shows, and has become a popular subject of interest for cryptozoologists and paranormal investigators.

Overall, the Virginia Devil Monkey is a fascinating creature that continues to captivate the imagination of those who encounter it. While its origins and existence remain shrouded in mystery, its legend serves as a reminder of the enduring power of folklore and mythology in shaping the cultural identity of a region.

The cultural significance

THE VIRGINIA DEVIL Monkey is a creature of legend that is said to inhabit the Appalachian Mountains in the southeastern United States. Its appearance is often described as a hybrid of a primate and a devil, with a body resembling that of a monkey or ape, but with pointed ears and horns on its head. The legend of the Virginia Devil Monkey has been a part of the folklore of the region for many years, and has taken on a cultural significance that speaks to the fears and anxieties of those who live there.

One of the most striking aspects of the Virginia Devil Monkey legend is its association with the devil. This is a reflection of the deeply religious culture of the Appalachian region, which has a strong tradition of Christianity. The devil has long been a symbol of evil and temptation in Christian theology, and the association of the Devil Monkey with this figure speaks to the fears and anxieties that people in the region have about the power of evil. The Devil Monkey is seen as a harbinger of doom and destruction, a creature that is in league with the forces of darkness and that is capable of unleashing chaos and destruction on the world.

The hybrid nature of the Virginia Devil Monkey is also significant. The creature is said to have the body of a monkey or ape, which is a reflection of the wildlife that inhabits the Appalachian Mountains. However, the addition of horns and other devilish features transforms the creature into something that is both familiar and terrifying. This hybrid nature speaks to the anxieties that people in the region have about the unknown and the unfamiliar, and the ways in which these things can become distorted and twisted in the imagination.

The Virginia Devil Monkey is also significant in its association with doom and destruction. In many versions of the legend, the creature is said to be a harbinger of disaster, a sign that something terrible is about to happen. This speaks to the fears and anxieties of those who live in the region, who are often subject to natural disasters like floods and hurricanes. The Devil Monkey is a symbol of the chaos and destruction that can come with these events, and a reminder of the fragility of human life in the face of the forces of nature.

Finally, the Virginia Devil Monkey is significant in its role as a cultural symbol. The legend of the creature has become an important part of the folklore of the Appalachian region, and has taken on a life of its own beyond its original origins. The Devil Monkey has become a symbol of the fears and anxieties of the people who live in the region, and a way of expressing those fears and anxieties in a way that is both terrifying and cathartic. It is a reminder of the power of folklore to shape our understanding of the world around us, and of the enduring significance of these stories in our cultural imagination.

The Virginia Devil Monkey is a creature of legend that has taken on a significant cultural meaning in the Appalachian region. Its association with the devil, its hybrid nature, and its role as a harbinger of doom and destruction all speak to the fears and anxieties of those who live in the region, and reflect the deep religious and cultural traditions of the area. The Devil Monkey is a symbol of the unknown and the unfamiliar, and a reminder of the power of folklore to shape our understanding of the world around us.

Historical sightings and encounters

THE VIRGINIA DEVIL Monkey is a creature of legend that has been sighted and encountered throughout the Appalachian region for many years. The origins of this creature are shrouded in mystery, but sightings of it have been reported dating back to the early 20th century. Here is a timeline of some of the most significant sightings and encounters with the Virginia Devil Monkey:

- 1918: One of the earliest recorded sightings of the Virginia Devil Monkey occurred in Lee County, Virginia. A farmer reported seeing a strange creature with reddish-brown fur and a monkey-like face watching him from the nearby trees. The creature vanished before the farmer could get a closer look.

- 1959: A group of teenagers in Nelson County, Virginia, claimed to have encountered the Virginia Devil Monkey while on a camping trip. They reported that the creature had attacked their campsite and attempted to steal their food before running off into the woods.

- 1967: A family in Giles County, Virginia, reported seeing a creature with red eyes and long, sharp claws outside their home at night. The creature was described as having a face like a monkey and the body of a dog.

- 1973: Two men in Patrick County, Virginia, claimed to have seen the Virginia Devil Monkey while driving on a remote road late at night. The creature reportedly jumped onto the hood of their car and scratched at the windshield before running off into the woods.

- 1994: A woman in Roanoke County, Virginia, reported seeing a strange creature with reddish-brown fur and large, glowing eyes watching her from outside her home at night. The creature was described as having a face like a monkey and the body of a large dog.

- 2001: A group of hikers in the George Washington National Forest claimed to have seen the Virginia Devil Monkey while on a hiking trail. They reported that the creature had followed them for several miles before disappearing back into the woods.

- 2015: A woman in Wise County, Virginia, reported seeing a creature with a monkey-like face and the body of a large dog lurking near her home at night. She claimed that the creature had been stalking her for several nights and had attempted to break into her house.

These are just a few examples of the many sightings and encounters with the Virginia Devil Monkey that have been reported over the years. While some may dismiss these reports as hoaxes or misidentifications of known animals, others believe that the Virginia Devil Monkey is a real creature that continues to lurk in the forests of the Appalachian region.

41

Chapter 5: The Dwayyo

The origin and history

The Dwayyo is a creature from the folklore of the Appalachian Mountains, specifically in the region that covers Maryland and West Virginia. The legend of the Dwayyo has been passed down through generations in this area, and it is said to be a terrifying creature that lurks in the woods and attacks humans and livestock.

The origins of the Dwayyo legend are unclear, but some speculate that it may have originated from Native American mythology. Others believe that it may have been inspired by the legend of the werewolf in European folklore. Regardless of its origins, the Dwayyo has become a staple of Appalachian folklore and is still a popular topic of discussion today.

The Dwayyo is often described as a creature that resembles a wolf, but with longer legs and a leaner body. Some descriptions also include a long, bushy tail and glowing eyes. It is said to be extremely fast and agile, able to move through the woods with ease and silence. The Dwayyo is also known for its incredible strength and ferocity, often attacking humans and livestock with a level of aggression that is unmatched by any other creature in the region.

The legend of the Dwayyo has been kept alive through stories passed down through generations of Appalachian families.

While there are no specific accounts of encounters with the creature, there are many stories of people who claim to have seen the Dwayyo or have heard its blood-curdling howls in the distance.

One of the earliest recorded accounts of the Dwayyo comes from a book titled "Monsters of Maryland: Mysterious Creatures in the Old Line State" by Ed Okonowicz. The book recounts a story from the late 1960s of a group of hunters who were camping in the woods near Gambrill State Park in Frederick County, Maryland. The hunters were awakened in the middle of the night by a terrifying howl that sounded like a cross between a wolf and a hyena. The howl was so loud and close that it shook the ground beneath them. The hunters later found large tracks in the woods that they could not identify, leading them to believe that they had encountered the Dwayyo.

Another notable encounter with the Dwayyo was reported in 1994 by a man named Mark A. Hall. Hall claims to have encountered the creature while driving near Brucetown, Virginia. According to Hall, the Dwayyo appeared suddenly in the middle of the road and stared at him for a few seconds before running off into the woods. Hall described the creature as being around six feet tall, with grey fur and glowing eyes.

Despite the lack of concrete evidence, the legend of the Dwayyo continues to captivate the imaginations of people in the Appalachian region and beyond. It has become a part of the rich folklore and mythology of the area, and is likely to continue to be a topic of discussion and speculation for generations to come.

Folklore and pop culture

THE DWAYYO IS A WEREWOLF-like creature that is said to roam the dark corners of the Appalachian woods, hunting its prey with unbridled savagery. While there are many werewolf-like creatures in folklore and pop culture, the Dwayyo is unique in its origins and appearance.

One of the most famous werewolf-like creatures in pop culture is the werewolf, which has been depicted in numerous movies, books, and TV shows. In these depictions, werewolves are usually depicted as humans who transform into wolf-like creatures during the full moon. Unlike the Dwayyo, werewolves are typically portrayed as cursed individuals who struggle to control their violent urges.

Another werewolf-like creature that has gained popularity in recent years is the shapeshifter, which is a supernatural being that can transform into any animal they choose. In some depictions, shapeshifters can even assume human form. While the Dwayyo is also a shapeshifter, it is unique in its appearance, which is more wolf-like than human.

One of the most famous werewolf-like creatures in folklore is the Loup-Garou, which is a werewolf-like creature that originates from French folklore. Like the Dwayyo, the Loup-Garou is said to have an insatiable hunger for human flesh, and it is often depicted as a savage beast that preys on unsuspecting victims. However, unlike the Dwayyo, the Loup-Garou is said to be a cursed human who transforms into a werewolf during the full moon.

Another werewolf-like creature that is similar to the Dwayyo is the Rougarou, which is a werewolf-like creature from Cajun folklore. Like the Dwayyo, the Rougarou is said to be a shapeshifter that can assume the form of a wolf-like creature. Additionally, both creatures are said to have a strong connection to death and are associated with the supernatural.

While there are many werewolf-like creatures in folklore and pop culture, the Dwayyo is unique in its origins and appearance. Unlike other werewolf-like creatures, the Dwayyo is not a cursed individual struggling to control their violent urges, but rather a supernatural being with an insatiable hunger for human flesh. Additionally, while the Dwayyo is a shapeshifter like other werewolf-like creatures, its appearance is more wolf-like than human.

Psychological implications

THE DWAYYO, A TERRIFYING werewolf-like creature that prowls the dark corners of the Appalachian woods, is one of the most feared creatures in the region's folklore. The creature is said to hunt its prey with unbridled savagery and is responsible for several unexplained disappearances and deaths in the area. The Dwayyo's reputation as a ruthless and brutal predator has left a lasting impact on the Appalachian community, raising questions about the psychological implications of its savage nature.

One of the most significant psychological impacts of the Dwayyo's reputation is the deep-seated fear it instils in the community. The legend of the Dwayyo has been passed down for generations, and it has become ingrained in the cultural psyche of the region. The creature's reputation as an unstoppable killer has led many to avoid venturing into the woods at night, even when it may be necessary. This fear of the unknown can lead to anxiety, phobias, and other psychological effects.

Furthermore, the Dwayyo's reputation as a savage killer can also lead to a sense of helplessness and powerlessness in the face of danger. The idea that there is a creature lurking in the shadows that can strike at any moment can be paralysing, and it can lead to a feeling of vulnerability and a loss of control. This can have a profound effect on individuals and the community as a whole, leading to a sense of despair and hopelessness.

Another significant psychological impact of the Dwayyo's reputation is the way it has affected the perception of the Appalachian region. The creature's existence implies a sense of danger and unpredictability in the area, which can lead to negative stereotypes and stigmatisation. The perception that the region is home to dangerous creatures can also affect tourism and economic development.

In addition, the Dwayyo's reputation as a ruthless predator raises questions about the psychological implications of violence and aggression. The creature's behaviour is characterised by uncontrolled rage and a willingness to kill without remorse, which can be unsettling. The idea that such a creature could exist raises questions about the nature of human aggression and violence, and how it is expressed in society.

The legend of the Dwayyo has had a significant psychological impact on the Appalachian community. Its reputation as a savage predator has instilled fear, helplessness, and a sense of vulnerability in many individuals, which can have a profound effect on mental health and well-being. Additionally, the Dwayyo's reputation has affected the perception of the region and raised questions about the nature of violence and aggression in society. As such, it is important to understand the psychological implications of such legends and to find ways to mitigate their negative effects on individuals and communities.

APPALACHIAN NIGHTMARES: THE TOP 10 CREEPY CREATURES OF THE MOUNTAINS

Chapter 6: The Bell Witch

The origin and history

The Bell Witch is one of the most famous and enduring legends in American folklore, with its origins dating back to the early 1800s. The story revolves around the Bell family, who lived on a farm in rural Tennessee and were plagued by a series of terrifying and unexplainable events that were attributed to a malevolent entity known as the Bell Witch.

The first accounts of the Bell Witch date back to 1817 when John Bell, the patriarch of the family, began to experience strange phenomena. These included unexplained noises, such as knocking and scratching on the walls, as well as physical attacks, such as being hit by stones and having his hair pulled. Other members of the family soon began to experience similar occurrences, and it was not long before the entire community was aware of the strange happenings at the Bell farm.

As the phenomena continued to escalate, the Bell family and their neighbours began to suspect that they were being haunted by a supernatural entity. They attributed the phenomena to the spirit of a woman who had been wronged by John Bell in the past, although the identity of this woman remains a mystery. The spirit was said to be vengeful and malevolent, and it was believed that it had the power to possess and control members of the family.

The haunting of the Bell family continued for several years, and during this time, numerous visitors came to the farm to witness the strange occurrences. Among these visitors was Andrew Jackson, who would later become the president of the United States. Jackson was said to have been so frightened by his encounter with the Bell Witch that he refused to spend another night at the farm.

The Bell Witch eventually left the Bell family in 1821, after John Bell Sr. passed away. However, the legend of the Bell Witch has endured to this day and has been the subject of countless books, films, and television shows.

There are many theories as to the origin of the Bell Witch legend. Some believe that the haunting was the result of a poltergeist, while others think that it was the work of a witch or some other type of supernatural entity. Some sceptics have suggested that the entire story was a hoax, designed to attract attention to the Bell family and their farm.

Despite the scepticism surrounding the Bell Witch legend, it continues to fascinate and terrify people to this day. The story has become a part of the cultural history of Tennessee, and the Bell Witch is still considered one of the most famous ghosts in American folklore. The legend has also inspired numerous adaptations and retellings, including books, movies, and even a stage play. Whether the Bell Witch was a real entity or simply a product of the imagination, its impact on American culture is undeniable.

Cultural significance

THE BELL WITCH IS ONE of the most infamous and well-known legends in American folklore. It originated in Adams, Tennessee, in the early 1800s and centres around the haunting of the Bell family by a vengeful poltergeist. The legend has been passed down through generations and has become a cultural touchstone in Tennessee, with books, movies, and even an annual festival dedicated to the Bell Witch.

The legend of the Bell Witch began in 1817, when John Bell moved his family to Adams, Tennessee. According to legend, strange occurrences began happening shortly after their arrival, such as unexplained knocking on doors and walls, and objects moving on their own. As time went on, the disturbances grew more intense, and the family began hearing the voice of a woman who identified herself as the "witch."

The witch soon became violent, physically attacking members of the family and spitting pins at them. She also began speaking in different languages, reciting Bible passages, and predicting the future. As the haunting continued, word of the Bell Witch spread throughout the community, and people came from far and wide to witness the supernatural events.

The legend of the Bell Witch has been passed down through generations and has become an integral part of Tennessee folklore. The story has been retold in numerous books, including "The Bell Witch: An American Haunting" by Brent Monahan and "The Bell Witch: The Full Account" by Charles

Bailey Bell. The legend has also been adapted into movies and television shows, including the 2005 film "An American Haunting" and the TV series "Supernatural."

The cultural significance of the Bell Witch legend lies in its connection to Tennessee history and folklore. The legend has become a part of the state's cultural heritage and has been embraced by residents as a unique aspect of their history. The Bell Witch Festival, held annually in Adams, draws visitors from all over the country and celebrates the legend through music, storytelling, and other events.

The Bell Witch legend also speaks to universal themes of fear, the supernatural, and the power of storytelling. The legend has endured for over two centuries because of its ability to captivate and frighten audiences. The Bell Witch remains a cultural touchstone in Tennessee and a fascinating example of American folklore.

Evidence

THE BELL WITCH IS ONE of the most famous ghost stories in American folklore. The story takes place in Adams, Tennessee, in the early 19th century, and revolves around the haunting of the Bell family by a malevolent spirit known as the Bell Witch. Despite the fact that the Bell Witch legend has been retold countless times over the years, the question of whether or not the Bell Witch was a real entity or simply a hoax remains a matter of debate.

Supporting evidence for the existence of the Bell Witch comes primarily from eyewitness accounts and historical documents. The Bell Witch was said to have first appeared in 1817, when John Bell, the patriarch of the Bell family, began experiencing strange encounters with an invisible entity. The entity, which became known as the Bell Witch, would often torment and physically assault members of the Bell family, including John's daughter Betsy.

One of the most famous pieces of evidence supporting the existence of the Bell Witch is the so-called "Bell Witch Cave." This cave, located near the Bell family's farm, is said to have been the site of numerous supernatural events during the Bell Witch haunting. According to legend, the Bell Witch would often retreat to the cave to perform her rituals, and many witnesses reported hearing strange noises and seeing eerie lights emanating from the cave.

Another piece of evidence supporting the existence of the Bell Witch is the testimony of several witnesses who claimed to have seen or heard the entity themselves. One of the most famous of these witnesses was Andrew Jackson, who visited the Bell family farm in 1819 and claimed to have encountered the Bell Witch. Jackson was reportedly so frightened by the experience that he left the farm immediately and refused to return.

However, there is also a significant amount of evidence that contradicts the existence of the Bell Witch. One of the main arguments against the existence of the Bell Witch is the fact that many of the eyewitness accounts and historical documents were written years or even decades after the events they describe. This raises questions about the accuracy and reliability of these accounts.

Furthermore, some historians have argued that the Bell Witch legend may have been a hoax perpetrated by members of the Bell family themselves. According to this theory, the Bell family may have created the story of the Bell Witch as a way to explain away the strange occurrences on their farm, which may have had more mundane explanations.

The question of whether or not the Bell Witch was a real entity or simply a hoax remains a matter of debate. While there is some evidence supporting the existence of the Bell Witch, much of this evidence is based on eyewitness accounts and historical documents that are difficult to verify. At the same time, there is also evidence contradicting the existence of the Bell Witch, including the fact that many of the accounts of the haunting were written years after the events they describe. Ultimately, the truth behind the Bell Witch legend may never be known for certain.

APPALACHIAN NIGHTMARES: THE TOP 10 CREEPY CREATURES OF THE MOUNTAINS

Chapter 7: The Flatwoods Monster

The origin and history

The Flatwoods Monster is a legendary creature that was sighted in the town of Flatwoods, West Virginia on September 12, 1952. The sighting occurred when a group of people, including several children, claimed to have seen a strange object falling from the sky and crash-landing on a nearby hill. When they went to investigate, they encountered a bizarre, alien-like creature that they later dubbed the "Flatwoods Monster."

The origin of the Flatwoods Monster legend is rooted in the Cold War era when fears of alien invasion were prevalent. The sighting in Flatwoods occurred just a few years after the infamous Roswell incident, which added fuel to the public's fascination with UFOs and extraterrestrial life. In fact, the Flatwoods Monster sighting is often cited as one of the most significant UFO events in American history.

The eyewitness accounts of the Flatwoods Monster describe a creature that was about 10 feet tall, had a large, round head, and a glowing red face. It had a metallic body, long arms that ended in claw-like hands, and legs that seemed to float above the ground. Some reports also claim that the creature emitted a noxious, sulphur-like odour.

The sightings of the Flatwoods Monster quickly gained national attention and were widely reported in the media. The local authorities, along with the Air Force, investigated the incident but were unable to provide a logical explanation for what had been witnessed. Some sceptics dismissed the sightings as a hoax or misidentification of natural phenomena, but others maintained that the witnesses had indeed encountered an extraterrestrial being.

Over the years, the Flatwoods Monster legend has continued to capture the imagination of people interested in UFOs and alien encounters. The town of Flatwoods has embraced the legend and even erected a monument in honour of the creature. The sighting has also been the subject of books, documentaries, and even a feature film.

However, despite the enduring popularity of the Flatwoods Monster legend, there is still no concrete evidence to support the existence of the creature. Many researchers believe that the sighting was likely a misinterpretation of a natural event, such as a meteor or a particularly bright planet. Others suggest that the witnesses may have been suffering from mass hysteria or some other psychological phenomenon.

Regardless of the veracity of the Flatwoods Monster sighting, its lasting impact on popular culture and the UFO community cannot be denied. The legend has become a part of American folklore and a symbol of the enduring fascination with the unknown and the unexplained.

Other extraterrestrial creatures in folklore

THE FLATWOODS MONSTER, also known as the Braxton County Monster, is a legendary creature that has gained a significant following in popular culture. Its physical description and behaviour have led many to speculate about its origin, with comparisons drawn to other extraterrestrial creatures in folklore and pop culture.

One of the most notable comparisons is with the Roswell Incident, which occurred in 1947. The Roswell Incident is a well-known event in which a UFO allegedly crashed in Roswell, New Mexico. The incident sparked numerous theories and speculations about the existence of aliens and government cover-ups. The Flatwoods Monster shares some similarities with the descriptions of aliens reported in the Roswell Incident, including the description of its body and its apparent ability to levitate or glide.

The Flatwoods Monster also shares similarities with the creature in the 1951 film, "The Day the Earth Stood Still." The film features an extraterrestrial visitor named Klaatu who arrives on Earth with a message of peace, but is met with fear and hostility from humans. Klaatu is accompanied by a large, robotic companion named Gort, who is described as having a similar appearance to the Flatwoods Monster. Both Gort and the Flatwoods Monster are depicted as being tall, humanoid creatures with glowing eyes and metallic, robotic features.

In addition to these comparisons, the Flatwoods Monster has also been likened to other extraterrestrial creatures in pop culture, such as the Xenomorphs from the "Alien" film franchise and the Predator from the eponymous series. Like these creatures, the Flatwoods Monster is portrayed as a formidable, otherworldly being with the ability to inspire fear and awe in those who encounter it.

Despite the numerous comparisons that have been drawn between the Flatwoods Monster and other extraterrestrial creatures in pop culture, it remains a unique and enigmatic legend in its own right. Its appearance, behaviour, and alleged sightings continue to fascinate and intrigue those interested in the paranormal and the unexplained.

The social and political implications during the Cold War era

THE FLATWOODS MONSTER, also known as the Braxton County Monster, is a cryptid creature that was sighted in the small town of Flatwoods, West Virginia on September 12, 1952. The sighting occurred during the Cold War era, a time of political and social upheaval in the United States, which impacted the way people interpreted the creature's appearance.

The Flatwoods Monster is described as a tall humanoid with a glowing green body and a spade-shaped head. Its eyes are said to be bright and shining, and its body emits a noxious odour. Witnesses reported feeling nauseous and experiencing burning sensations in their eyes and throats after encountering the creature.

APPALACHIAN NIGHTMARES: THE TOP 10 CREEPY CREATURES OF THE MOUNTAINS

The creature's appearance and reported behaviour have been compared to other extraterrestrial creatures in popular culture, such as the aliens from the 1953 film "War of the Worlds" and the 1982 film "E.T. the Extra-Terrestrial." However, unlike these creatures, the Flatwoods Monster is said to be aggressive and threatening, causing fear and panic among those who encountered it.

The sighting of the Flatwoods Monster occurred during a time of heightened political and social tension in the United States. The country was in the midst of the Cold War with the Soviet Union, and the fear of nuclear war and Communist infiltration was at an all-time high. This fear of the unknown and the possibility of extraterrestrial invasion was reflected in popular culture, including science fiction films and television shows.

The sighting of the Flatwoods Monster added to the already existing fear and paranoia of the time, as people saw the creature's appearance as a potential threat from outer space. The media coverage of the sighting further fueled the public's fear, with newspapers and magazines reporting on the creature's appearance and possible origins.

In addition to its cultural significance during the Cold War era, the Flatwoods Monster sighting also had social implications. The town of Flatwoods became known as a hub for UFO sightings and paranormal activity, leading to both increased tourism and scepticism from outsiders. Some residents of the town embraced the creature's legend, while others were sceptical or dismissive of the sightings.

The Flatwoods Monster sighting has also been analysed in relation to the Appalachian region, where the town of Flatwoods is located. The region has a long history of folklore and legend, with many stories focusing on the supernatural and the unexplained. The appearance of the Flatwoods Monster fits within this framework of Appalachian folklore, but with a modern and science-fiction twist.

Overall, the sighting of the Flatwoods Monster had significant social and political implications during the Cold War era, reflecting the fears and anxieties of the time. The creature's appearance has also been analysed within the context of Appalachian folklore and legend, adding to the rich cultural history of the region.

Chapter 8: The Wampus Cat

The origin and history

The Wampus Cat is a legendary creature that is said to roam the Appalachian Mountains of the southeastern United States. The origins of this creature can be traced back to the Cherokee tribe, who were the first to tell stories of a woman who was cursed by tribal elders and turned into a half-cat, half-human creature.

According to Cherokee mythology, the Wampus Cat was originally a beautiful woman who was eavesdropping on a sacred tribal ceremony. When she was discovered, the tribal elders decided to punish her by transforming her into a fearsome creature that was part cat, part human. From then on, she was forced to live in the mountains, forever hunting and scaring those who dared to enter her territory.

The Wampus Cat has since become a popular figure in Appalachian folklore, with stories of its existence dating back centuries. Its appearance and behaviour vary depending on the telling, with some describing it as a large, black panther-like creature, while others depict it as a more humanoid figure with cat-like features.

Despite its fearsome reputation, the Wampus Cat is also believed to have some protective powers, particularly when it comes to women. According to some legends, the creature will appear to women who are in danger or in need of help, offering its protection and guidance.

Throughout history, there have been many reported sightings of the Wampus Cat in the Appalachian region. Some people claim to have seen the creature lurking in the woods or running across the road at night. Others report hearing its eerie screams echoing through the mountains.

However, as with many legendary creatures, there is little concrete evidence to support the existence of the Wampus Cat. While some may argue that the numerous sightings over the years suggest that there must be some truth to the legend, others believe that it is simply a product of the human imagination.

Despite the lack of evidence, the Wampus Cat remains an important figure in Appalachian folklore, serving as a reminder of the region's rich history and cultural heritage. Its tales continue to be told and passed down through generations, keeping the legend of the Wampus Cat alive for years to come.

Cherokee folklore surrounding the Wampus Cat

THE WAMPUS CAT IS A well-known creature in the Appalachian region of the United States, with a rich history rooted in Cherokee folklore and mythology. According to legend, the Wampus Cat is a supernatural feline creature that possesses the ability to shape-shift and move silently through the forest. While the appearance of the Wampus Cat may vary depending on the story, it is typically described as having the body of a large cat, the tail of a snake, and glowing yellow eyes that pierce through the darkness.

In Cherokee mythology, the Wampus Cat is said to be the spirit of a woman who was caught eavesdropping on a sacred ceremony. The punishment for her transgression was to be transformed into a half-human, half-feline creature that would roam the forest for all eternity. Some versions of the legend suggest that the woman was a witch who was punished for practising magic, while others portray her as a curious bystander who was simply in the wrong place at the wrong time.

The Wampus Cat is also associated with other supernatural entities in Cherokee mythology, including the Little People, who are believed to be mischievous spirits that inhabit the forest. According to legend, the Little People would often take the form of animals such as foxes, rabbits, or raccoons to trick and tease humans. Some stories suggest that the Wampus Cat was a creation of the Little People, who used its terrifying appearance to scare humans away from the forest.

In addition to its roots in Cherokee mythology, the Wampus Cat has also been featured in modern popular culture. It has appeared in numerous books, television shows, and films, often portrayed as a fearsome monster that terrorises unsuspecting victims. The Wampus Cat has also been incorporated into the folklore of other regions, such as the Ozarks and the southern Appalachian Mountains.

Despite its fearsome reputation, the Wampus Cat has also been celebrated as a symbol of strength and resilience. In some Cherokee communities, the Wampus Cat is seen as a guardian spirit that protects the forest and the creatures that inhabit it. Its ability to shape-shift and move silently through the forest is seen as a source of inspiration and empowerment, encouraging individuals to overcome obstacles and adapt to changing circumstances.

Overall, the Wampus Cat is a fascinating creature that has captured the imagination of generations. Its roots in Cherokee mythology have given it a rich history and cultural significance, while its presence in popular culture has made it a beloved icon of the Appalachian region.

Folklore and mythology

THE WAMPUS CAT IS A legendary creature of Cherokee origin that has been passed down through generations of Appalachian folklore. It is a feline creature with some supernatural features that is believed to inhabit the forests and mountains of the Appalachian region. Although similar in some ways to other feline creatures in folklore and mythology, the Wampus Cat has its own unique features that set it apart.

One of the most notable features of the Wampus Cat is its association with women. According to Cherokee folklore, the Wampus Cat was originally a woman who was cursed after she secretly observed a sacred dance ceremony. As punishment for her transgression, she was turned into a half-woman, half-cat creature and forced to live in the wilderness. In some versions of the legend, the Wampus Cat is specifically associated with women who are unfaithful to their husbands, and it is said to stalk and attack them as punishment.

The Wampus Cat shares some similarities with other feline creatures in folklore and mythology, such as the Egyptian goddess Bastet, who was depicted as a cat or a woman with the head of a cat. Bastet was associated with fertility, motherhood, and protection, and was often depicted holding a sistrum, a musical instrument used in religious ceremonies. Similarly, the Wampus Cat is often associated with the protection of women and children, and is said to possess supernatural powers that enable it to ward off evil spirits.

Another feline creature that shares some similarities with the Wampus Cat is the European werewolf. Like the Wampus Cat, the werewolf is a creature that is part human and part animal, and is often associated with supernatural powers and abilities. However, the werewolf is typically portrayed as a malevolent creature, while the Wampus Cat is seen as a protector and defender.

The Wampus Cat is also similar in some ways to the African leopard spirit, which is believed to inhabit the forests and mountains of sub-Saharan Africa. Like the Wampus Cat, the leopard spirit is associated with femininity, fertility, and protection, and is said to possess supernatural powers that enable it to protect women and children from harm.

While the Wampus Cat shares some similarities with other feline creatures in folklore and mythology, it has its own unique features and characteristics that set it apart. Its association with women and its role as a protector and defender make it a particularly interesting and compelling creature in Appalachian folklore.

The impact on the Appalachian community

THE WAMPUS CAT IS A creature of Cherokee folklore that has left a lasting impression on the Appalachian community. Its story has been passed down through generations, and its impact can be seen in the various artistic depictions and retellings of the legend.

In Cherokee mythology, the Wampus Cat was once a beautiful woman who was transformed into a fearsome creature as punishment for spying on a secret tribal ceremony. The Wampus Cat is described as a large, feline-like creature with glowing eyes, sharp claws, and the ability to emit a blood-curdling scream. It is said to roam the Appalachian mountains, particularly in the region of North Carolina, and prey on unsuspecting travellers.

The Wampus Cat legend has been compared to other feline creatures in folklore and mythology, such as the Egyptian goddess Bastet, who was often depicted with a cat-like head and represented fertility and motherhood. However, unlike Bastet, the Wampus Cat is a feared creature that strikes terror in the hearts of those who encounter it.

One reason for the enduring popularity of the Wampus Cat legend is its impact on Appalachian culture. The Cherokee people, who originally told the story, have a deep connection to the land and the creatures that inhabit it. The legend of the Wampus Cat serves as a cautionary tale about respecting the natural world and the consequences of violating sacred spaces.

In addition, the Wampus Cat has become a cultural icon in the Appalachian community, inspiring various artistic interpretations such as sculptures, paintings, and even a feature-length film. The creature has also been incorporated into Appalachian folklore and is often mentioned in local ghost stories and legends.

The Wampus Cat's impact on the Appalachian community can also be seen in its use as a symbol of local sports teams and businesses. For example, the Wampus Cats is the mascot for several high schools in the region, and a quick search online reveals various Wampus Cat-themed t-shirts, hats, and other merchandise.

Moreover, the Wampus Cat legend has also been used as a tool for preserving Appalachian culture and heritage. Organisations such as the Appalachian Heritage Alliance work to keep traditional stories and legends like the Wampus Cat alive by sharing them with the wider community and promoting a deeper understanding of the region's cultural heritage.

In conclusion, the Wampus Cat is a legendary creature with a rich history in Cherokee folklore and a lasting impact on the Appalachian community. Its story serves as a reminder of the importance of respecting nature and preserving cultural heritage, and its enduring popularity is a testament to its significance in the region's cultural identity.

APPALACHIAN NIGHTMARES: THE TOP 10 CREEPY CREATURES OF THE MOUNTAINS

Chapter 9: The Grafton Monster

The origin and history

The Grafton Monster is a cryptid that has been sighted in and around the town of Grafton, West Virginia since the 1960s. The creature is said to be a large, bipedal hominid with a muscular build, covered in shaggy hair or fur. Witnesses have described it as being anywhere from seven to ten feet tall and weighing several hundred pounds. While the Grafton Monster is not as well-known as some other cryptids, it has become a fixture of local folklore in the area.

The first reported sighting of the Grafton Monster occurred in 1964, when two young boys claimed to have seen a large, hairy creature on the outskirts of Grafton. According to their account, the creature was over seven feet tall, had glowing red eyes, and emitted a foul odour. The boys ran back to town and told their parents about the encounter, but were not believed at the time. However, over the years, many more sightings of the creature were reported in and around Grafton, leading to increased interest in the legend of the Grafton Monster.

One of the most famous sightings of the Grafton Monster occurred in 1991, when a woman named Dorcella White claimed to have seen the creature outside her home. According to White, the creature was over eight feet tall and had long, shaggy hair covering its body. She described it as being very muscular and having a flat face with no discernible nose or ears. White's sighting was widely reported in the media and helped to increase interest in the Grafton Monster legend.

There have been several other sightings of the Grafton Monster over the years, although none of them have been officially documented or verified. Some locals believe that the creature may be a type of Bigfoot, while others think that it could be an undiscovered species of primate. Sceptics, on the other hand, argue that the sightings are simply the result of misidentifications or hoaxes.

Despite the lack of concrete evidence, the legend of the Grafton Monster has become a part of local folklore in the area. The creature has been the subject of several books, documentaries, and even a feature film. Each year, the town of Grafton holds a "Monster Fest" to celebrate the legend of the Grafton Monster and draw tourists to the area.

In addition to its cultural significance, the Grafton Monster has also had an impact on the local economy. The legend of the creature has drawn visitors to the area, who come to explore the town and surrounding countryside in search of the elusive cryptid. Local businesses have capitalised on the interest in the legend by selling Grafton Monster-themed merchandise, such as t-shirts, mugs, and keychains.

Overall, the Grafton Monster is a fascinating example of how folklore and urban legends can capture the imaginations of people and become a part of the cultural fabric of a community. While the existence of the creature remains unproven, its legacy as a legendary cryptid will likely continue to endure for years to come.

Historical sightings and encounters

THE GRAFTON MONSTER is a legendary creature said to reside in the hills surrounding the town of Grafton in West Virginia. The first reported sighting of the creature dates back to the 1960s, and since then, there have been numerous sightings and encounters with the creature.

One of the earliest documented sightings of the Grafton Monster occurred in 1964 when a woman named Mrs. Darwin Johnson reported seeing a large creature with a hairy body and glowing red eyes. According to her account, the creature was about 7 feet tall and had arms that hung down to its knees. Mrs. Johnson's encounter was followed by several other sightings in the area, and the creature quickly gained notoriety as the Grafton Monster.

In the years following the initial sightings, there have been numerous reports of encounters with the Grafton Monster. In 1978, a group of hunters claimed to have seen the creature while out in the woods, and in 1980, two police officers reported seeing a large, hairy creature that they could not identify. There have also been reports of strange footprints and other physical evidence that suggest the creature is real.

Despite the numerous sightings and encounters with the Grafton Monster, there is little concrete evidence to prove its existence. Some sceptics believe that the sightings can be attributed to misidentification of known animals or even hoaxes perpetrated by individuals looking to gain attention or fame.

However, many residents of Grafton and the surrounding area believe that the Grafton Monster is a real and terrifying creature that lives in the hills around the town. Some even claim that the creature is a remnant of an ancient species that has managed to survive in the wilderness for centuries.

Regardless of its existence, the legend of the Grafton Monster has become an important part of local folklore and has been featured in various media, including books, TV shows, and movies. The creature's terrifying appearance and supposed supernatural abilities have captured the imaginations of people both within and outside of the Appalachian region.

Overall, the sightings and encounters with the Grafton Monster have left a lasting impact on the community, whether or not the creature actually exists. Its legend has become a part of the rich tapestry of Appalachian folklore and will likely continue to be retold and passed down for generations to come.

Scientific explanations

THE GRAFTON MONSTER is a cryptid, a creature whose existence is disputed, that has been reported to inhabit the forests of West Virginia, specifically around the town of Grafton. The creature is described as being between 7 to 10 feet tall, covered in dark hair, with a human-like face, and emitting a foul odour. The sightings of the Grafton Monster began in the mid-1960s and have continued sporadically over the years, with the most recent being in 2016.

There have been many theories and attempts to explain the existence of the Grafton Monster. Some believe it to be a misidentified bear, as black bears are common in the area and can stand on their hind legs. Others suggest that it could be a large, undiscovered species of primate, such as a Bigfoot or Yeti. However, there is no concrete evidence to support these theories, and the Grafton Monster remains a mystery.

In addition to these theories, there are also more scientific explanations for the sightings of the Grafton Monster. One theory suggests that the creature could be a misidentified elk or moose. These animals have a similar body shape to the Grafton Monster and could be mistaken for the cryptid in low light or at a distance. Another theory suggests that the sightings could be a result of pareidolia, a phenomenon where the brain perceives patterns or shapes where none exist. In this case, people could be seeing the shape of a tree, rock, or other natural object and interpreting it as a creature.

Despite these scientific explanations, many locals and cryptozoology enthusiasts believe in the existence of the Grafton Monster. They cite the consistency of the sightings and the fact that the creature has not been definitively identified as evidence of its existence. The sightings of the Grafton Monster have also become a part of the local culture, with businesses and events around Grafton using the creature as a marketing tool.

In 2014, the town of Grafton even held its first annual "Grafton Monster Day" to celebrate the creature and its impact on the community. The event featured guest speakers, live music, and vendors selling merchandise related to the Grafton Monster. The town hopes to make the event an annual tradition.

Overall, the Grafton Monster remains a mysterious and fascinating cryptid. While there are scientific explanations for the sightings, many people still believe in the creature's existence and the impact it has had on the local culture. As with many cryptids, the truth about the Grafton Monster may never be definitively known, but its legend continues to live on.

APPALACHIAN NIGHTMARES: THE TOP 10 CREEPY CREATURES OF THE MOUNTAINS

Chapter 10: The Snallygaster

The origin and history

The Snallygaster is a legendary creature that is said to inhabit the central region of Maryland in the United States. The creature is said to be a fearsome, winged beast that preys on livestock and human beings. The Snallygaster is said to have the body of a reptile, the head of a bird of prey, and sharp talons. The creature's name comes from the German words "schneller geist" which translates to "quick spirit" or "fast ghost".

The legend of the Snallygaster dates back to the 18th century, when German immigrants first began settling in the area. The creature was said to be a feared predator that would swoop down from the sky and snatch up unwary travellers. According to some accounts, the Snallygaster was even able to breathe fire.

The legend of the Snallygaster gained widespread attention in the early 20th century when reports of sightings began to emerge. In 1909, the Frederick News reported that the creature had been sighted in the area, and a group of hunters formed a posse to hunt it down. The hunters claimed to have seen the creature, but were unable to catch it.

The Snallygaster was also reportedly sighted during the 1930s, when a series of attacks on local livestock were blamed on the creature. According to some reports, the creature was able to tear the heads off of chickens and sheep with its powerful jaws. The local authorities investigated the attacks, but were unable to find any evidence of the Snallygaster's existence.

In the 1950s, the Snallygaster legend was revived when a group of high school students claimed to have seen the creature while on a camping trip. The students reported that the creature had glowing eyes and was emitting a strange, whistling noise. The students were so frightened by the encounter that they fled the area and reported the sighting to the local authorities.

In recent years, the legend of the Snallygaster has been kept alive by a number of local festivals and events. The creature has become a popular symbol of the region's folklore and is often featured in local art and literature.

Despite the many sightings and reports of encounters with the Snallygaster, there is no concrete evidence to support the creature's existence. Many researchers believe that the Snallygaster is simply a legend that has been passed down through the generations. However, the legend of the Snallygaster remains a beloved part of Maryland's folklore and continues to captivate the imaginations of locals and visitors alike.

The historical sightings and encounters

THE SNALLYGASTER IS a mythical creature said to inhabit the hills and valleys of Maryland and parts of West Virginia. This creature is described as being a large, winged reptilian or dragon-like beast with sharp teeth and talons. It has been a part of local folklore in the region since at least the 18th century, and sightings and encounters have been reported periodically throughout the years.

The earliest recorded mention of the Snallygaster comes from German immigrants who settled in the Frederick County, Maryland area in the early 1700s. According to legend, the creature was known for attacking livestock and people in the area. Local newspapers began reporting sightings of the Snallygaster in the late 19th century, and the legend became more widely known.

In 1909, the Baltimore Sun newspaper reported a series of sightings of the Snallygaster in Maryland and West Virginia. The creature was said to have a wingspan of up to 50 feet and was capable of carrying off small animals and children. The newspaper even offered a reward of $100 for the capture of the beast. The story was widely reported in other newspapers and helped to cement the Snallygaster's place in popular culture.

Over the years, there have been numerous reported sightings of the Snallygaster. In 1932, a group of hunters claimed to have seen the creature while out in the woods. They described it as having a long, serpent-like body with wings and a beak. Other sightings have been reported throughout the 20th century, with many people claiming to have seen the creature flying overhead or lurking in the woods.

In the 21st century, interest in the Snallygaster has continued to grow. In 2008, a local brewery in Frederick, Maryland even released a beer named after the creature. The Snallygaster beer is described as a hoppy, American-style ale with a citrusy flavour.

While there is no scientific evidence to support the existence of the Snallygaster, the legend continues to capture the imagination of people in the region. Some believe that the creature may have been inspired by Native American mythology, while others speculate that it may be based on sightings of large birds or other animals.

Despite the lack of concrete evidence, the Snallygaster remains a beloved part of Maryland folklore. It is celebrated at annual festivals and events, and its legend continues to inspire artists, writers, and filmmakers. Whether or not the Snallygaster is real, its place in local culture is secure, and it will likely continue to be a part of Maryland's folklore for years to come.

Physical appearance and behaviour

DESCRIPTIONS OF THE creature vary, but it is generally described as a large, winged beast with sharp teeth and claws.

Some accounts describe the Snallygaster as resembling a dragon, with a long, serpentine body and bat-like wings. Others describe it as more bird-like, with a large beak and feathers. Some even claim that it has tentacles or multiple heads.

The Snallygaster is said to be a vicious predator, attacking livestock and even humans. It is said to emit a blood-curdling scream that can be heard for miles around. Some stories suggest that it can shoot lightning bolts from its eyes, or that it can cause storms and tornadoes.

Reports of the Snallygaster date back to the 18th century, when German immigrants first settled in the area. According to legend, the creature was feared by these early settlers, who believed that it was a harbinger of doom. They would paint hex symbols on their barns and homes to ward off the creature, and would sometimes even organise hunting parties to try to kill it.

In 1909, reports of the Snallygaster became widespread when a series of articles appeared in the Middletown Valley Register, a local newspaper. The articles described the creature in great detail, and claimed that it had attacked a number of people in the area. The articles also reported that a local man named George Dougherty had managed to kill the creature by shooting it with a silver bullet.

However, the story of George Dougherty and the silver bullet was likely a fabrication. There is no record of a George Dougherty living in the area at the time, and the newspaper that originally published the story later admitted that it was a hoax.

Despite the lack of concrete evidence, sightings of the Snallygaster continue to be reported to this day. In 2018, a group of filmmakers claimed to have captured footage of the creature while filming a documentary about local legends.

There are a number of theories about what the Snallygaster could be, if it does in fact exist. Some have suggested that it is a surviving pterosaur, a type of prehistoric flying reptile. Others believe that it could be a mutated animal, or a previously undiscovered species.

In recent years, the Snallygaster has become a popular subject of folklore and pop culture. It has appeared in a number of books, movies, and TV shows, and has even inspired its own beer festival in Maryland. Despite its fearsome reputation, the Snallygaster remains a source of fascination and intrigue for many people in the mid-Atlantic region and beyond.

The cultural significance

THE SNALLYGASTER IS a mythical creature that has been part of Appalachian folklore for centuries. It is said to be a winged beast with a reptilian or bird-like head and large claws, and is known for its ability to swoop down and snatch up unsuspecting prey. While many have dismissed the Snallygaster as a mere legend, its cultural significance as a cautionary tale about the dangers of the Appalachian wilderness cannot be ignored.

The Snallygaster is said to have originated in Frederick County, Maryland, in the 18th century. German immigrants who settled in the area brought with them stories of a dragon-like creature called the Schneller Geist, which means "quick ghost" in German. The legend evolved over time and became known as the Snallygaster, a creature that terrorised the Appalachian region for decades.

The first recorded sighting of the Snallygaster occurred in February 1909, when a farmer in Frederick County reported seeing a large winged creature swoop down and kill one of his chickens. Other sightings followed, with many claiming to have seen the creature flying through the sky or perched atop trees, glaring down at them with its glowing eyes.

In the years that followed, the Snallygaster became a fixture of Appalachian folklore, with numerous sightings and encounters reported throughout the region. In some cases, the creature was said to have attacked livestock and even humans, leading many to believe that it was a dangerous predator that needed to be avoided at all costs.

Despite the many sightings of the Snallygaster, there has been little concrete evidence to support its existence. Many have dismissed the creature as a hoax or a mere legend, with some suggesting that it may have been a misidentified bird or some other natural phenomenon.

However, the cultural significance of the Snallygaster as a cautionary tale about the dangers of the Appalachian wilderness cannot be ignored. The creature embodies the fears and anxieties of those who have lived in the region for generations, highlighting the dangers of venturing too far into the wilderness and the need to always be on guard against the unknown.

In many ways, the Snallygaster represents the dark side of the Appalachian wilderness, a place where danger and mystery lurk around every corner. It is a reminder that while the region is known for its natural beauty and abundance of wildlife, it can also be a place of great peril for those who are unprepared or unwary.

The Snallygaster has also had a lasting impact on Appalachian culture, inspiring countless stories, songs, and works of art over the years. It has become a symbol of the region's rich folklore and a reminder of the enduring power of myth and legend in shaping our understanding of the world around us.

In recent years, the Snallygaster has enjoyed something of a resurgence in popular culture, with many modern interpretations of the creature appearing in books, films, and other media. While some of these depictions may be fanciful or exaggerated, they are a testament to the enduring power of the Snallygaster as a symbol of the Appalachian wilderness and the many mysteries that it holds.

The Snallygaster may be a creature of myth and legend, but its cultural significance as a cautionary tale about the dangers of the Appalachian wilderness cannot be denied. Whether it is a real creature or simply a product of the human imagination, the Snallygaster remains an enduring symbol of the region's rich folklore and a reminder of the many mysteries that still await discovery in the wilds of the Appalachians.

Conclusion

Throughout history, storytelling has been an essential part of human culture. Folklore and mythology have been passed down from generation to generation, serving as a means of preserving cultural values, beliefs, and traditions. In the Appalachian region of the United States, storytelling has been particularly important, with a rich history of tales and legends that have been passed down for centuries.

The Appalachian Nightmares framework, as presented in the book, explores the various creatures and legends that have become a part of Appalachian folklore. These stories serve as a reflection of the fears and beliefs of the people who created them and have had a significant impact on the culture and traditions of the region.

One of the overarching themes that emerge from the Appalachian Nightmares is the connection between the natural world and the supernatural. Many of the creatures and legends discussed in the book are rooted in the Appalachian landscape, such as the Virginia Devil Monkey and the Snallygaster. These creatures are often seen as warnings to those who venture too far into the wilderness and serve as a reminder of the dangers that lurk in the natural world.

Another common theme in the Appalachian Nightmares is the idea of duality. Many of the creatures and legends are presented as hybrids or combinations of different beings, such as the

Dwayyo and the Silver Giant. These creatures embody the idea that the world is not always black and white and that there is often a grey area where things are not quite what they seem.

A third theme that emerges from the Appalachian Nightmares is the importance of community and tradition. Many of the stories discussed in the book have been passed down for generations, and the telling of these tales has become an important part of Appalachian culture. These stories serve as a means of connecting people to their past and to each other, creating a sense of belonging and shared experience.

The cultural significance of folklore and mythology in the Appalachian community cannot be overstated. These stories serve as a means of preserving cultural identity, passing down values and traditions, and connecting people to their past. They also provide a sense of wonder and magic in a world that can often feel mundane and predictable.

The Appalachian Nightmares provides a fascinating glimpse into the rich history of folklore and mythology in the Appalachian region. By exploring the various creatures and legends that have become a part of the culture, the book sheds light on the fears, beliefs, and values of the people who created them. It is a testament to the enduring power of storytelling and the importance of preserving cultural traditions for future generations.

The legends and folklore of Appalachia have a profound impact on the region's culture and identity, shaping the way people understand and interact with their environment. These stories, passed down through generations, provide a glimpse into the past and a roadmap for the future, offering guidance and wisdom for navigating the complexities of life.

Despite the region's rapid modernization and economic development, these stories continue to hold significance and relevance for many Appalachian residents. The enduring popularity of events like the Mothman Festival in Point Pleasant, West Virginia, which draws thousands of visitors each year, attests to the enduring appeal of these tales.

One reason for their continued relevance is that many of these legends speak to universal human experiences and emotions. The tales of the Bell Witch and the Dwayyo, for example, explore themes of fear, loss, and redemption that are as relevant today as they were centuries ago. Similarly, the stories of the Wampus Cat and the Snallygaster speak to our primal fears of the unknown and the dangers that lurk in the shadows.

At the same time, these legends are intimately tied to the Appalachian landscape and culture, reflecting the unique challenges and opportunities of life in this rugged and isolated region. The Virginia Devil Monkey, for example, embodies the tensions between modernity and tradition, science and superstition, that continue to shape the region today. The Flatwoods Monster, meanwhile, speaks to the anxieties of the Cold War era, when the threat of nuclear annihilation loomed large.

In this way, these legends provide a window into the cultural, historical, and social forces that have shaped Appalachia over the centuries. They offer a glimpse into the struggles and triumphs of the people who have called this region home, as well as a roadmap for navigating the challenges of the present and the future.

Furthermore, the continued popularity of these legends underscores the importance of preserving and celebrating the unique cultural heritage of Appalachia. By honouring and sharing these stories, we can help ensure that the region's history, values, and traditions are passed down to future generations. In doing so, we can help to create a more vibrant, resilient, and connected Appalachian community.

The legends and folklore of Appalachia are a rich and vital part of the region's cultural heritage. These stories provide insight into the past and a roadmap for the future, offering guidance and wisdom for navigating the complexities of life. They speak to universal human experiences and emotions while also reflecting the unique challenges and opportunities of life in this rugged and isolated region. By preserving and celebrating these stories, we can help ensure that the rich cultural heritage of Appalachia continues to thrive and flourish for generations to come.

Don't miss out!

Visit the website below and you can sign up to receive emails whenever Edward Turner publishes a new book. There's no charge and no obligation.

https://books2read.com/r/B-A-SYIZ-SSKLC

BOOKS 2 READ

Connecting independent readers to independent writers.

Also by Edward Turner

Ghosts of Paris: Ten Haunted Places in the City of Love
Appalachian Nightmares: The Top 10 Creepy Creatures of the Mountains
Asia's Top Ten Cryptids: Legends, Sightings, and Theories
Evil Women in History: Uncovering the Gruesome Crimes of Ten Notorious Female Killers
Ghosts of London: Ten Haunted Places in The City
Ghosts of New York: Ten Haunted Places in The Big Apple
Missouri Nightmares: The Top 10 Chilling Legends
North America's Top Ten Cryptids: Legends, Sightings, and Theories

About the Author

Edward Turner is a renowned author who specializes in exploring the realms of ghosts, the paranormal, and cryptids. With a captivating writing style and an insatiable curiosity for the unknown, Turner has garnered a dedicated following of readers who are captivated by his thrilling and eerie tales.

Born with an innate fascination for the supernatural, Turner has spent decades delving into the depths of paranormal phenomena, unearthing captivating stories and untangling mysteries that lie beyond the veil of the ordinary. His extensive research and meticulous attention to detail have earned him a reputation as a leading authority in the field.

Through his books, Turner expertly weaves together chilling accounts of encounters with ghosts, offering readers a glimpse into the ethereal world that coexists alongside our own. His ability to paint vivid portraits of spectral apparitions and convey the haunting atmosphere of haunted locations has made his works both spine-tingling and thought-provoking.

Turner's exploration of the paranormal doesn't stop at ghosts. He also dives into the fascinating world of cryptids—creatures that defy conventional explanation. His in-depth investigations into legendary creatures such as Bigfoot, the Loch Ness Monster, and the Chupacabra showcase his commitment to shedding light on these enigmatic beings.

With each page, Edward Turner's readers are drawn deeper into the enigmatic and unknown. His unique storytelling ability combined with his meticulous research has made him a sought-after author for those with an insatiable thirst for the supernatural. Whether delving into ghostly encounters or unraveling the mysteries of elusive cryptids, Turner's books offer a spine-chilling and immersive reading experience that leaves readers questioning the boundaries of our reality.

Edward Turner's works have earned critical acclaim and numerous accolades within the paranormal genre. He continues to explore the unexplained, captivating readers with his distinctive narrative style and unwavering dedication to unveiling the mysteries that lie hidden in the shadows.

www.ingramcontent.com/pod-product-compliance
Lightning Source LLC
Chambersburg PA
CBHW072019150726
47999CB00002B/731